W0113794

better together*

* This book is best read together, grownup and kid.

 **akidsco.com**

a kids
book
about

a kids book about

FIRST-GENERATION IMMIGRANTS

by Travis Chen

A Kids Co.
Editor Emma Wolf
Designer Rick DeLucco
Creative Director Rick DeLucco
Studio Manager Kenya Feldes
Sales Director Melanie Wilkins
Head of Books Jennifer Goldstein
CEO and Founder Jelani Memory

DK
Delhi Technical Team Bimlesh Tiwary Pushpak Tyagi, Rakesh Kumar
Senior Production Editor Jennifer Murray
Senior Production Controller Louise Minihane
Senior Acquisitions Editor Katy Flint
Acquisitions Project Editor Sara Forster
Managing Art Editor Vicky Short
Managing Director, Licensing Mark Searle

First American edition, 2025
Published in the United States by DK Publishing, 1745 Broadway, 20th Floor,
New York, NY 10019

First published in Great Britain in 2025 by
Dorling Kindersley Limited, 20 Vauxhall Bridge Road, London SW1V 2SA
A Penguin Random House Company

The authorised representative in the EEA is
Dorling Kindersley Verlag GmbH. Arnulfstr. 124, 80636 Munich, Germany

Copyright © 2025 Dorling Kindersley Limited
A Kids Book About, Kids Are Ready, and the colophon 'a' are trademarks of A Kids Book About, Inc.
10 9 8 7 6 5 4 3 2 1
001-349917-May/2025
All rights reserved.
No part of this publication may be reproduced, stored in or introduced into a retrieval system,
or transmitted, in any form, or by any means (electronic, mechanical, photocopying, record ng,
or otherwise), without the prior written permission of the copyright owner.

A catalog record for this book is available from the Library of Congress.
A CIP catalogue record for this book is available from the British Library.
ISBN: 978-0-2417-4375-1

DK books are available at special discounts when purchased in bulk for sales
promotions, premiums, fund-raising, or education use. For details, contact:
DK Publishing Special Markets, 1745 Broadway, 20th Floor, New York, NY 10019
SpecialSales@dk.com

Printed and bound in Slovakia
www.dk.com
akidsco.com

MIX
Paper | Supporting
responsible forestry
FSC™ C018179

This book was made with Forest
Stewardship Council™ certified
paper – one small step in DK's
commitment to a sustainable future.
Learn more at www.dk.com/uk/
information/sustainability

This book is dedicated to Mom and Dad, who worked tirelessly to bring my 2 sisters, Mio and Monica, and me to the United States for a brighter future.

Despite the struggles that first-generation immigrants like us face, we overcame them all.

Intro
for grownups

What does it mean to leave your home and move someplace new, not understanding any of the local language or culture, yet trying to get by? The answer is complex for many, but one thing most first-generation immigrant families want is to feel accepted—and, ultimately, to feel at home.

While the first-generation immigrant experience is unique, many people relate to the whirlwind of finding their identity. For some, it takes years to fully appreciate their background and culture, and to embrace their cultural customs.

Yet, there's comfort in understanding that we, first-generation immigrants, are not alone. Many immigrants across the world have similar experiences and relatable stories to share. And when we're able to communicate these common struggles, the world grows just a bit closer.

I remember moving into
a house with nothing in it.

No toys, no furniture, no thing which felt familiar to me.

I was upset that I had to move to a new place. But my parents moved here to pursue the **American dream.**

BETTER WO
BETTER EDU
AND MORE
OPPORTUNI

RK,
CATION,
TIES.

My family are first-generation immigrants.

And being a first-generation immigrant is not easy.

It involves a lot of emotions, self-discovery, and learning how to fit into a new culture.

A **first-generation immigrant** is someone who left their home country to come to a new country.

For me, I moved from Taiwan

**to America with my family
when I was 3 years old.**

My parents made that decision
because they wanted the best
for me and my siblings.

Any time you move to a new environment is hard.

But I felt lucky to have my family with me. **They gave me a sense of support and home during a big transition.**

AND WHAT A TRANSITION THAT WAS.

When I started school,
I didn't understand English,
so I had a lot of
catching up to do.

Every day, I arrived at school a little earlier than my classmates for extra instruction, so I could better understand and speak with them, up until the 4th grade.

I worked hard to understand English as well as the students around me.

Even still, there were a few words I struggled with. (English is a super hard second language to learn!)*

*Think about the word "read." Sometimes it sounds like "reed," and sometimes it sounds like "red." What's up with that?!

I felt lonely because I didn't fit in with the rest of the kids.

I also faced discrimination because I was different from the kids around me.

I brought Asian foods for lunch, like dumplings, and some of the other kids made fun of me, saying they smelled like cat food.

This was the food I ate at home with my family, and I couldn't understand why kids were teasing me for it.

To me, food is central to our sense of identity. It also brings people closer together.

But it made me feel ashamed, like I was doing something wrong.

So much so that I went home and begged my parents to pack American snacks like the ones my classmates ate.

I WISH I KNEW AT THE TIME THAT THERE WAS NOTHING WRONG WITH ME OR THE FOOD I BROUGHT TO SCHOOL.

It would have been awesome
if the kids around me chose to
take the opportunity to get to
know me and my culture.

One of the hardest things about being a **first-generation immigrant** is discovering your identity and who you truly are.

Growing up in America,
I wanted a different skin color
or hair color so I could fit
in with other kids.

I thought changing those parts
of who I am would help me
make more friends and relate*
more to the people around me.

The truth is,

WHERE YOU CO
IMPORTANT PART

ME FROM IS AN
OF WHO YOU ARE.

Your identity is like a puzzle, made up of all the things that make you special.

It's not just about who you are, but also the values and experiences from other cultures that make you unique.

I still celebrate Lunar New Year with my family. This means a lot of food and a lot of the color red, which represents good luck and fortune.

And on birthdays, I eat noodles because in my culture, noodles represent having...

A LONG AND HEALTHY LIFE.

The things I value that I learned from my culture will always be part of me.

Things like working hard, being humble, having resiliency*, respecting elders, and understanding where you come from.

*Resiliency means that when you experience a setback, you're able to get up, learn from it, and keep going toward your goals.

The values that make me the person I am are things that have been passed down for generations.

As a kid, I didn't always appreciate who I was because it was really hard to be different.

Maybe you feel the same way, and I understand how difficult that is.

But as a grownup, I'm grateful for the things that make me unique.

You are shaped by your cultural roots and the culture you inherit.

And that isn't always easy to embrace.

When I'm in Taiwan, I'm
"TOO AME

and when I'm in America, I'm
"TOO TAIW

RICAN,"

ANESE."

People will ask me,
"So, where's home?"

When I tell them Los Angeles,
the response is usually,
"But where are you *really* from?"

Sometimes it feels like
nowhere is home for me.

And that hurts...a lot.

Living with 2 cultures can feel like playing tug-of-war, but it's also a

SUPERI

POWER!

That's because I can understand and relate to people from both parts of myself.

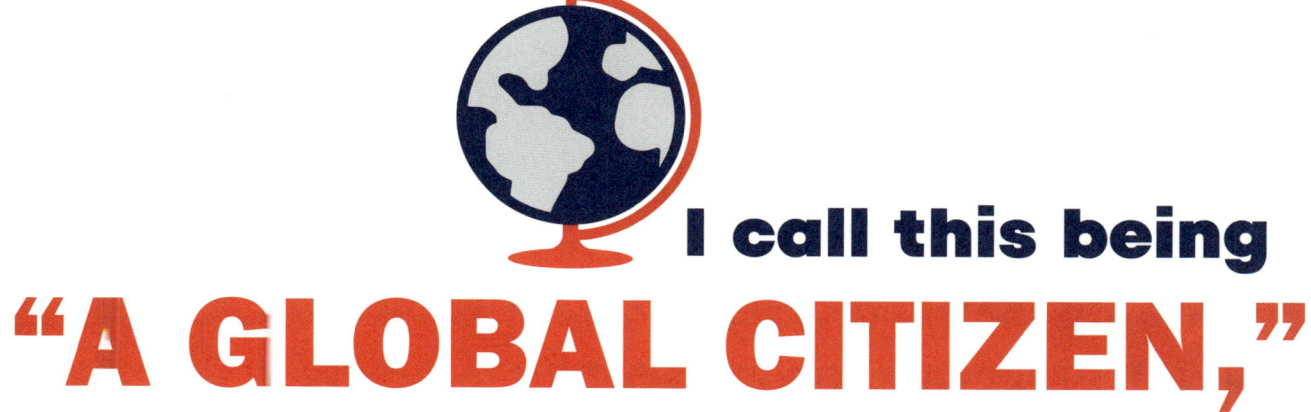

I call this being **"A GLOBAL CITIZEN,"** which means understanding different cultures and connecting with people across the world.

My world is so much **BIGGER**

because of all the cultures I inhabit.

I remind myself that being a **first-generation immigrant** is something to celebrate!

YOU ARE UNIQUE. YOU ARE SPECIAL. AND YOU ARE THE EXPERT OF YOUR STORY.

You are a part of a community of people who see you, understand you, and can relate to your experience.

But you're also not alone.

So the next time you bring dumplings to school, remember that it is OK to be fully you.

You belong here and deserve to celebrate who you are.

BE PROUD TO BE A FIRST-GENERATION IMMIGRANT.

I know I am.

Outro
for grownups

Being a first-generation immigrant is a lifelong journey—the adversities and challenges don't stop as you grow up. But it helps when this community is able to come together and shed light on the full experience of moving to a foreign country, not knowing the cultural customs, language, food, or way of doing things.

And yes, the mental health effects that come with being a first-generation immigrant are deep and wide. Living with 2 or more cultures can often feel like playing tug-of-war...and struggling to win. But, embrace this experience as a superpower and remind yourself that being a first-generation immigrant is something to celebrate.

You are unique. You are special. And you are not alone.

About The Author

Travis Chen (he/him) wrote this book for all first-generation kids. Having moved to a new environment at the age of 3 with no toys, no furniture, and nothing that felt familiar to him, he knows this transition is no easy task.

Faced with discrimination for honoring his cultural traditions at school and in the workplace, Travis felt ashamed. But he knows that his Taiwanese and Asian American identity is what makes him unique. Today, he celebrates his culture with pride.

This book is meant to highlight the adversity that first-generation immigrants face daily in their lives. It is also meant to show kids who are struggling with their cultural identities that being a global citizen is pretty cool and brings the world closer together.

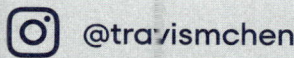 @travismchen   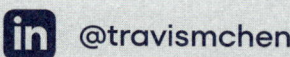 @travismchen   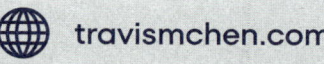 travismchen.com

Made to empower.

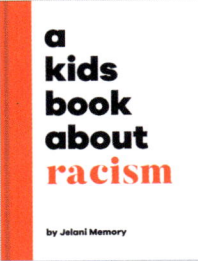

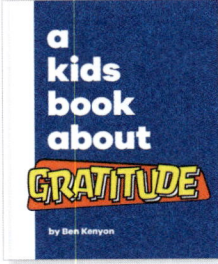

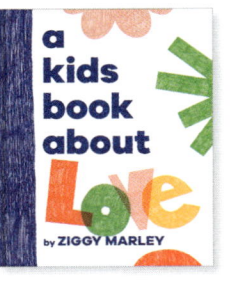
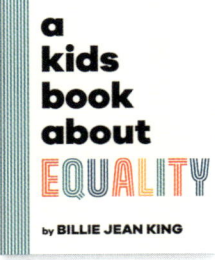

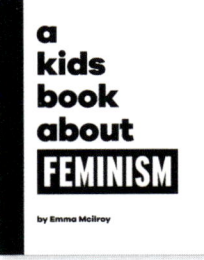
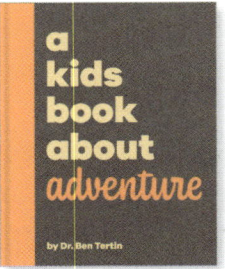
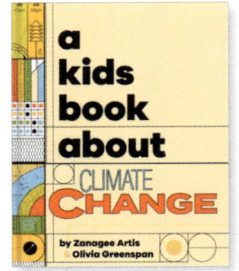

Discover more at akidsco.com